- **Expressions From Northern Ireland**
Edited by Michelle Afford

 Young Writers
First published in Great Britain in 2006 by:
Young Writers
Remus House
Coltsfoot Drive
Peterborough
PE2 9JX
Telephone: 01733 890066
Website: www.youngwriters.co.uk

All Rights Reserved

© Copyright Contributors 2005

SB ISBN 1 84602 367 X

Foreword

Young Writers was established in 1991 and has been passionately devoted to the promotion of reading and writing in children and young adults ever since. The quest continues today. Young Writers remains as committed to the fostering of burgeoning poetic and literary talent as ever.

This year's Young Writers competition has proven as vibrant and dynamic as ever and we are delighted to present a showcase of the best poetry from across the UK. Each poem has been carefully selected from a wealth of *Playground Poets* entries before ultimately being published in this, our thirteenth primary school poetry series.

Once again, we have been supremely impressed by the overall high quality of the entries we have received. The imagination, energy and creativity which has gone into each young writer's entry made choosing the best poems a challenging and often difficult but ultimately hugely rewarding task - the general high standard of the work submitted amply vindicating this opportunity to bring their poetry to a larger appreciative audience.

We sincerely hope you are pleased with our final selection and that you will enjoy *Playground Poets - Expressions From Northern Ireland* for many years to come.

Contents

Brooklands Primary School, Belfast
Lewis Thompson (9)	1
Jessica Markwell (10)	2
Kenneth Watson (9)	3
Aisling McMullan (9)	4
Daniel Crawford (9)	5
Catherine Ewen (9)	6
Adam Patterson (9)	7
Katie Brown (8)	8
Adele Walker (9)	9
Jenna Daley (8)	10
Louise Magill (8)	11
Holly Sloan (8)	12
Ryan Craig (8)	13
Charmaine Ennis (8)	14
Rebekah Rice (8)	15
Chloe McCullough (8)	16
Faith McCune (8)	17
Curtis Murray (8)	18
Courtney McCreedy (8)	19
Shannon Mitchell (9)	20
Matthew Lindsay (9)	21
Dylan Cairns (9)	22
Lauren Kirkwood (9)	23
Shannon Bell (10)	24
Shakeela Gill (10)	25
Alix Boyd (9)	26
Ryan Campbell (9)	27
David Magill (10)	28
Nikki Cousins (11)	29
Andrew Gorman (10)	30

Carrowreagh Primary School, Ballymoney
Julie Young (9)	31
Laura Monteith (8)	32
Emily Millar (8)	33
Stephanie Peacock (8)	34
Elaine McFadden (9)	35
Charlotte McManus (9)	36

Max Parker (8) — 37
David McAneaney (8) — 38
Ryan Moon (8) — 39
Leon Macartney (8) — 40
Zara Loughridge (9) — 41
Jill McCaughern (8) — 42
Christopher Campbell (9) — 43
Shannon Steele (8) — 44

Irvinestown Primary School, Irvinestown

Ciara Gill (8) — 45
William Graham (8) — 46
Rachel Pearson (9) — 47
Rachel Funston (9) — 48
Adam Kerrigan (8) — 49
Maeve Gallagher (7) — 50
Rhys Foster (8) — 51
Connor Keys (7) — 52
Emma Glover (8) — 53
Alexander Dean (8) — 54
Matthew Thompson (7) — 55
Steven Johnston (9) — 56
Rachel Law (7) — 57
Peter Elliott (8) — 58
Joshua Crozier (7) — 59
Holly Johnston (10) — 60
Amy Richmond (10) — 61
Jonathan Boomer (10) — 62
Edel Gallagher (10) — 63
Mark Wilson (11) — 64
Henry McCarthy (10) — 65
Debbie Keys (9) — 66
Emma Boomer (9) — 67
Stewart Quinn (10) — 68
Lana Knox (9) — 69
Graeme Read (9) — 70
Jane Funston (9) — 71
Danielle Walker (10) — 72
Maeve McCann (8) — 73
David Knox (9) — 74
Mark Miller (9) — 75

Daryl Holden (8) 76
Rebecca Gray (9) 77
Holly Walker (9) 78
Nathan Richmond (10) 79
Scotty Thompson (11) 80

Mount St Catherine's Primary School, Armagh
Claudia Kelly (8) 81
Nadine Murtagh (8) 82
Emma Kelly (8) 83
Abigail Quigley (9) 84
Eimear Grimley (9) 85
Maureen O'Hara (9) 86
Catherine Marley (8) 87

St Joseph's Primary School, Crossgar
Órla Reavey (8) 88
Dervla McCormick 89
Donal O'Toole (7) 90
Niamh McErlane (8) 91
Christopher Martin (7) 92
Daniel Martin 93
Aileen Mahon (7) 94

St Martin's Primary School, Garrison
Lisa Galligan (9) 95
Thomas McHugh (9) 96
Kilian Gilroy (11) 97
Ruth Leonard (9) 98
Clodagh Treacy (9) 99
Roisin Flanagan (9) 100
Gillian Carson (10) 101
Ruairí Maguire (10) 102
Dan Keaney (10) 103
Rosemary McGowan (10) 104
Ciara Flanagan (9) 105
Katie Clancy (9) 106
Elaine Rooney (9) 107
Sarah Treacy (9) 108
Keith Keegan (9) 109

St Patrick's Primary School, Ballynahinch
Matthew Manley (9)	110
Keava Blaney (8)	111
Hannah Magowan (8)	112
Rachael Walsh (8)	113
Rachel Jones (8)	114
Cathryn Baker (8)	115
Nicole McKay (8)	116
Tara Orr (9)	117
Conor Smyth-Small (10)	118
Liam Doherty (10)	119
Katy Flanagan (9)	120
Ryan Molloy (9)	121
Natasha McMillan (10)	122

St Patrick's Primary School, Dungannon
Katie Hughes (7)	123
Carrie Coary (8)	124
Anna Maguire (7)	125
Peter Kelly (7)	126
Ciaran McAllister (7)	127
Chloe Fitzpatrick (7)	128
Dearbhla Rafferty (7)	129
Eoin O'Hagan (7)	130
Darryl Mullan (8)	131
Caoimhe Shields (8)	132
Cormac McGhee (7)	133
Toni Morris (7)	134
Callum Donnelly (7)	135
Donovan McNeil (8)	136
Aideen Duffy (7)	137
Philip Barrett (7)	138

SS Patrick & Brigid's Primary School, Ballycastle
Bebhinn Stuart (7)	139
Liam Fletcher (8)	140
Toraigh Watson (8)	141
Laura Duigan (8)	142
Émer McBride (7)	143
Eoin McCaughan (7)	144
Aisha McAuley (7)	145

Pearse Molloy (7)   146
Georgie Killough (7)   147
Bronagh Scullion (7)   148
Tiarnan Jennings (8)   149
Conor Mullan (7)   150
Caolan Hill (7)   151
Alex McMullan (7)   152
Chloe Woods (7)   153
Caitlin Winchborne (7)   154
Caoimhe Marie Donnelly (7)   155
Clodagh McFaul (7)   156
Ryan Davidson (8)   157
Cara Kinney (7)   158
Ben Large (8)   159
Caoimhe Norwood (7)   160
Cailín Haughey (7)   161
Patrick Bonnar (7)   162
Logan McLean (8)   163
Shannon McDermott (7)   164
Shannon McGrogan (7)   165
Ruthie Burns (7)   166

Towerview Primary School, Bangor
Mark Conroy (8)   167
Shannon Palnoch (7)   168
Hannah Tuson (8)   169
Phoebe Preston (7)   170
Nicholas Price (7)   171
Tamsyn Cummins (7)   172
Lucy Blaney (7)   173
Melanie Sloan (7)   174
Connor Firth (7)   175
Rhiannon Wells (8)   176
Nathan James Connor Ritchie (8)   177
Jordan Thompson (7)   178
Joshua Doherty (7)   179
Rebecca McCormick (10)   180
Erin Rachel Moore (10)   181
Sara McDowell (10)   182
Portia Preston (10)   183
Ashleigh Phillips (10)   184

Paige Morrow (10)	185
India McPeak (9)	186
Thomas Watson (8)	187
Rachel Lyle (9)	188
Angus Gardiner (8)	189
Chloe Budd (10)	190
Nial Ian William Scott (8)	191
Israel Corry (8)	192
Jenny Huston (10)	193
Andrew Mellon (9)	194
Lee Puckrin (8)	195
Gemma McCamley (8)	196
Andrew Poxon (9)	197
Conor Dorrian (9)	198
Lucy McClenahan (9)	199
James Carson (10)	200
Alex Hannant (7)	201
Natasha Mellon (7)	202
Jack Maitland (7)	203
Zoë Elena Beckett (7)	204
Emma Waugh (7)	205
Matthew Adendorff (8)	206
James Wylie (7)	207
Dylan Robinson (7)	208
Savannah Romein (7)	209
Chloe Neill (7)	210
Ryan Scott (7)	211
Siân Barker (7)	212
Ben McCreery (7)	213
Catherine Poxon (8)	214
Isaac Cave (8)	215

The Poems

Autumn's Here

Leaves falling down,
maroon, russet, crimson, scarlet.
Walking down the street,
seeing farmers cut their fields.

I see it yellow, then it's cream,
I look down.
I see a multicoloured quilt,
over yucky creepy-crawlies.

You're looking straight at it,
then you see the dancing,
dying fluttering leaves.

Less animals about
because they're hibernating,
or birds because
they're migrating.

So autumn's here,
we say goodnight to summer!

Lewis Thompson (9)
Brooklands Primary School, Belfast

Leaves

Trees dying
leaves changing colour
to brown, crimson, russet and maroon
when they fall off
slowly fluttering
turning
twisting
down to the ground.
Children playing in them
crunching while they walk
squirrels scurrying to collect
nuts and berries.
While the sleepy hedgehog
sleeps in his
comfortable, patterned quilt.

Jessica Markwell (10)
Brooklands Primary School, Belfast

Hedgehogs

The big, crispy bed
Waits below
The hedgehog hides in
And waits for the glow
Of the sunshine he loves
Sometimes comes up for a nibble
Then goes back to sleep
In a multicoloured hiding place
It is like he plays
Hide-and-seek with Winter
But Spring always finds him.

Kenneth Watson (9)
Brooklands Primary School, Belfast

Leaves

Fighting hedgehogs
Buried under
The multicoloured leaves
Squirrels finding nuts and berries
Beside the sleepy trees
Maroon, orange, gold and brown
Leaves falling off the yawning trees.

Aisling McMullan (9)
Brooklands Primary School, Belfast

Autumn Oak Tree

I'm *really, really, really angry*
The leaves will not leave me alone
A powerful north-east wind
Forces the leaves down where they belong.

Dancing, fighting and fluttering
Turning russet, scarlet, crimson and gold
As they sleep on the ground.

The little mice are covered by a multicoloured blanket;
A safe warm home for them.
Playing in the crunchy, cracking,
Rustling and twisting leaves.

Daniel Crawford (9)
Brooklands Primary School, Belfast

Autumn Chases In

Summer fades away
Autumn starts to appear once again
As I stare out my window, the world changes
The green leaves fade to a rusty, crusty brown
And the berries turn red and black to fatten up the birds
The leaves gradually fall off the trees
Maroon, russet, orange, yellow and brown
Fluttering
Down
Down
Down
Crunch and crackle
They cry as we jump on them
Then they die
The green grass turns to a patterned carpet
Of scarlet, crimson and gold
Then the hedgehog comes along
And snuggles down to sleep.

Catherine Ewen (9)
Brooklands Primary School, Belfast

Autumn

A utumn leaves come tumbling down
U nderfoot, the leaves crunch
T he squirrels bury nuts underground
U nderground, hedgehogs hibernate
M any birds fly to warmer countries
N ext season is winter.

Adam Patterson (9)
Brooklands Primary School, Belfast

Autumn

A utumn is now here
U nderfoot, hedgehogs hibernate
T he farmer's crops are being harvested
U nder trees, squirrels collect nuts
M any people are wearing warmer clothes
N ext season is winter.

Katie Brown (8)
Brooklands Primary School, Belfast

Autumn

A utumn leaves come falling down
U nder branches, spiders weave their webs
T he farmer is harvesting his crops
U nderground, squirrels hide their nuts
M any birds fly to warmer countries
N ow autumn has come.

Adele Walker (9)
Brooklands Primary School, Belfast

Autumn

A utumn is now here
U nderground, the hedgehogs hibernate.
T he migrating season is starting,
U nderfoot the leaves go *crunch!*
M ums are getting out warmer clothes,
N ow autumn is ending and winter's coming.

Jenna Daley (8)
Brooklands Primary School, Belfast

Autumn

A utumn is now here,
U nderground, a hedgehog hibernates.
T he farmer harvests his crops,
U nderfoot, leaves crunch.
M any people wear warm jumpers.
N ext season will be winter.

Louise Magill (8)
Brooklands Primary School, Belfast

Autumn

A utumn is now here
U nderfoot, I stamp on leaves
T he farmers harvest their crops
U nder the ground, squirrels hide their nuts
M igrating birds fly overhead
N ow autumn has come to an end.

Holly Sloan (8)
Brooklands Primary School, Belfast

Autumn

A mazing coloured leaves tumble down,
U nderfoot, leaves crunch.
T he farmer is harvesting his crops,
U nderground, a hedgehog hibernates.
M any birds fly to warmer countries.
N ow it is autumn.

Ryan Craig (8)
Brooklands Primary School, Belfast

Autumn

A mong the leaves I jump and play
U nder our feet, leaves crunch.
T wirling leaves fall down,
U nder the trees, squirrels hide their nuts,
M any birds fly to warmer countries.
N ow we wear warmer clothes.

Charmaine Ennis (8)
Brooklands Primary School, Belfast

Autumn

A utumn is here now,
U nder the tree, squirrels are storing nuts.
T oday I saw some birds migrating,
U nderfoot, I crunch the leaves.
M any farmers harvest their crops.
N ext season is cold winter.

Rebekah Rice (8)
Brooklands Primary School, Belfast

Autumn

A mazing leaves come twirling down
U nderground, animals are hibernating.
T he farmer harvests his crops,
U nderground, the squirrels hide their nuts.
M igrating birds fly overhead,
N ext season is winter.

Chloe McCullough (8)
Brooklands Primary School, Belfast

Autumn

A utumn leaves come falling down,
U nderfoot are squirrels' nuts.
T oday the days are getting darker and shorter,
U nder the leaves, the spiders spin their webs.
M any birds migrate to warmer countries,
N ext season is winter.

Faith McCune (8)
Brooklands Primary School, Belfast

Autumn

A mong the leaves, squirrels hide their nuts,
U nder branches, spiders spin their webs.
T he farmer harvests his crops,
U nfortunately, the cold winter is coming.
M any birds gather to migrate,
N ow we wear warmer clothes.

Curtis Murray (8)
Brooklands Primary School, Belfast

Autumn

A ll the leaves come swirling down,
U nderground, squirrels hide their nuts.
T he migrating season is starting
U nder the ground are worms.
M ums and dads get fluffy coats,
N ow autumn is at the end. Look out, winter is coming!

Courtney McCreedy (8)
Brooklands Primary School, Belfast

Bizzie Bee

Bizzie Bee follow me,
To a place where you are free.
To a quiet place in the wood,
Away from danger, it will be good.
A hollow tree is where we'll meet,
With sweet honey inside, there is plenty to eat,
And quietly we will rest and enjoy a great day,
My newest best friend, don't fly away.

Shannon Mitchell (9)
Brooklands Primary School, Belfast

The Match

The whistle blows and off we go
The match gets under way
A strike for goal, a foul is given
'Come on Ref!' they say.

The ground is full, not a seat to be had
The fans wear blue and white
There are supporters waiting to get in
I hope they do not fight!

We're on the attack, our striker shoots
The ball hits the back of the net
The match is won, three points for us
But the league is not over yet!

Matthew Lindsay (9)
Brooklands Primary School, Belfast

Dogs

Dogs are loveable
Dogs are huggable
Dogs are helpful
Dogs are playful

Dogs bite and sometimes fight
And they sneak around at night
If they bite, I get a fright
And rush about and hide out of sight!

Dylan Cairns (9)
Brooklands Primary School, Belfast

Our Lollipop Man

Friday was a sad day in Brooklands Primary School,
Our lollipop man had to retire.
George, you were so cool.
You knew all the children's names,
And even all their mummies.
You always had a smile for all
And told us jokes, so funny.
It was a sad day when you left,
As lollipop men go, you're the best.
Brooklands was a safer place,
When you were on patrol.
To help us safely get to school,
That was always your goal.
We gave you lots of lovely gifts,
As you were a special man.
How on earth did you get them home?
Oh yes, you drive a van.
And now my poem has to stop,
George, you're the best with a lollipop!

Lauren Kirkwood (9)
Brooklands Primary School, Belfast

My Favourite Lollipop Man

There was a very happy man
Who was our very own lollipop man
Who stood in the wind and rain
And he knew every boy and girl's name
From Shannon to Vincent
And all the primary school infants
He watched us safely across the road
He sent us sweets from young to old
He was always there to say
How good you look today
Our George made us laugh, not cry
Until the day he said goodbye.

Shannon Bell (10)
Brooklands Primary School, Belfast

My Sister Jade

My sister Jade is 22 years old
And very pretty, I'm often told.
She cannot walk, she cannot see
She can't even play with me.
I comb her hair and help wash her face
I wouldn't have another sister to take her place.

Shakeela Gill (10)
Brooklands Primary School, Belfast

George

We had a lollipop man,
Who was the best in the land,
He looked after the girls and boys,
As if they were his precious toys.
You would always hear him shout,
'Don't run out, come here and give me your hand!'
He knew all us kids by name,
And the parents, just the same.
We have never seen him frown,
Nor look as if he was down.
He really loved his job,
Though it only paid a few bob.
We were sorry to see him go,
For we know he loved us so.
He kept us kids on our toes,
And watched as we grows.
It should have been 'grow',
But it doesn't rhyme,
But then, I'm only nine!

Alix Boyd (9)
Brooklands Primary School, Belfast

Hallowe'en

Coming soon is Hallowe'en
Where ghosts and ghouls will be seen.
I'll dress up like the winged Reaper
And from house to house, I'll be a creeper.
I'll dip my face into jelly
To find some money and fill my belly.
Then later on, when it gets darker
I'll finish the night with a firework and sparkler.

Ryan Campbell (9)
Brooklands Primary School, Belfast

Here I Am, Sitting In A Graveyard

Here I am, sitting in a graveyard
I'm wet, I'm cold
And I've nowhere to go.

Here I am, sitting in a graveyard
Reading all the headstones
Waiting for the sun.

Here I am, sitting in a graveyard
Here comes the undertaker
And I'm all alone.

Here I am, sitting in a graveyard
Talking to the undertaker
Then he pushes me in!

Here I am, lying in a coffin
He closes the lid
And I'm all alone.

Here I am, lying in a coffin
I'm lowered into the ground
'Let me out!'

David Magill (10)
Brooklands Primary School, Belfast

Winter Settings

Winter, winter, glorious winter
When the days get dark
And icicles are like splinters.

Snow, snow, glorious snow
So white it glows
When the wild winds blow.

Trees, trees, glorious trees
They lose all their leaves
And there are no more bees.

Heat, heat, glorious heat
You may choose to extract it by using peat
In other words, sit down on a seat
And warm your freezing, icy feet.

Nikki Cousins (11)
Brooklands Primary School, Belfast

A Winter's Day At The Harbour

The gulls are flying everywhere
The smell of sea salt in the air.
The noise of the wind rocking the boats
Fishermen huddled in their coats.
Grey skies forming, the rain pouring down
The beach is empty and no one's around.

Andrew Gorman (10)
Brooklands Primary School, Belfast

The Fascinating Horse

Beautiful
Galloping
Bucking
Horse
Bucking here, galloping there
Prancing all around.
Young, cute, white, little Bobby
Bobby
My pony, Bobby.

Julie Young (9)
Carrowreagh Primary School, Ballymoney

Koala Bears

Fluffy
Cute
Black noses
Slowly, gently climbing
Steadily, harmlessly
Like a fluffy bear
I love koalas so much
Koala bears
They're so tiny and cute
Koala bears.

Laura Monteith (8)
Carrowreagh Primary School, Ballymoney

Butterfly

Colourful
Pretty
Lovely
Butterfly
Flying high, flying low
Swooping
Like a moth in the sky
I am excited when I see you
Butterfly
Magnificent butterfly.

Emily Millar (8)
Carrowreagh Primary School, Ballymoney

Puppy

Brown eyes
Cute
They like to play
Always on the go.
Patch
All puppies like to play.
Unsteady,
He likes to go and get his ball and he's on the go.
Puppy
He's the best in the puppy world.

Stephanie Peacock (8)
Carrowreagh Primary School, Ballymoney

Kittens

Gentle
Furry
Sweet
Kitten
Pouncing for its food
Carefully
Happily
Like a little mouse
So sweet and soft, kitten
Kitten
Soft kitten.

Elaine McFadden (9)
Carrowreagh Primary School, Ballymoney

Horses

Strong
Fast,
Lovely,
Horses.
Strolling horses,
Cheerfully,
Happily,
Like the wind.
I love to hear your happy neighs.
Horses,
Bucking horses.

Charlotte McManus (9)
Carrowreagh Primary School, Ballymoney

Lion

Mighty
Powerful
Fast
Lion
Slaying its prey
Strong
Quiet
Stealthy
Like a BMW
Lion
Fast lion.

Max Parker (8)
Carrowreagh Primary School, Ballymoney

Snakes

Small
Green
Scaly
Snake
Slithering all day long
Slowly
Sliding
Like a small green stick
I would hate to see you upside down
Snake
Poisonous snake.

David McAneaney (8)
Carrowreagh Primary School, Ballymoney

Velociraptor

Powerful
Mighty
Fast
Velociroptor
Jumping on its prey
With strength
Powerfully
Like a small tank
I wish it was not extinct
Velociraptor
Speedy, powerful velociraptor.

Ryan Moon (8)
Carrowreagh Primary School, Ballymoney

Lion

Tough
Fast
Killing
Lion
Pouncing on its prey
Powerfully
Stealthily
Like a flash of lightning
I admire your power
Mighty
Killing lion.

Leon Macartney (8)
Carrowreagh Primary School, Ballymoney

Sasha The Puppy

Cute
Playful
Hungry
Puppy
Pouncing on her brother's tail
Sneakily
Cheekily
Like a playing robot
I would be sad if you died
Puppy
Yapping puppy.

Zara Loughridge (9)
Carrowreagh Primary School, Ballymoney

Monkeys

Funny
Cuddly
Slow
Monkeys
Swinging from tree to tree
Dancing
Scratching
Monkeys
Like a clown
I love watching your tricks
Monkeys, cheerful monkeys.

Jill McCaughern (8)
Carrowreagh Primary School, Ballymoney

Cow

Strong
Powerful
Mighty
Cow
Trotting all day long
Happily
Merrily
I would hate to see you on a plate
Cow
Mighty
Cow.

Christopher Campbell (9)
Carrowreagh Primary School, Ballymoney

Monkey

Climbing
Fast
Hiding
Monkey
Climbing from trees
Happily
Powerfully
Hiding in trees
Sad if you see a monkey lying dead
Monkey
Super monkey.

Shannon Steele (8)
Carrowreagh Primary School, Ballymoney

Dolphins

They can have a bottle nose,
They have sparkly, silvery skin,
They are big, little and medium.
They can jump up high,
They can leap out of the sky,
They can dance in the water and sleep in the current,
Dolphins, dolphins, dolphins,
I like dolphins.

Ciara Gill (8)
Irvinestown Primary School, Irvinestown

Dragonflies - Haiku

Up above the pond
Dazzling dragonflies hover
Wanting to lay eggs.

William Graham (8)
Irvinestown Primary School, Irvinestown

Cats

Cats, cats, cats
White, fluffy, soft cats
Fat, thin and podgy cats
Miaowing, purring, hissing cats
Hunting, stalking, killing cats
Cats, cats, cats.

Rachel Pearson (9)
Irvinestown Primary School, Irvinestown

Kittens

Kittens, kittens, kittens
Black, white and ginger kittens
Big, small and medium kittens
Playing, racing, running kittens
Purring, miaowing, licking kittens
Kittens, kittens, kittens.

Rachel Funston (9)
Irvinestown Primary School, Irvinestown

Quads

Quads, quads, quads
Red, blue, green quads
Big, small, medium quads
Quick, racing, chasing quads
Speeding, sliding, skidding quads
Quads, quads, quads.

Adam Kerrigan (8)
Irvinestown Primary School, Irvinestown

Mice

Mice, mice, mice
Small, fat and thin mice
Peeping, creeping, squeaking mice
Nibbling, gnawing, thieving mice
Mice, mice, mice.

Maeve Gallagher (7)
Irvinestown Primary School, Irvinestown

Apples - Haiku

Tucked in the orchard
Rosy red, yellow and green
Hanging on a branch.

Rhys Foster (8)
Irvinestown Primary School, Irvinestown

Dinosaurs

Dinosaurs, dinosaurs, dinosaurs
Lumpy, spiky, feathery dinosaurs
Gross, gigantic, tall dinosaurs
Munching, crunching, swiping dinosaurs
Swimming, running, fighting dinosaurs
Dinosaurs, dinosaurs, dinosaurs.

Connor Keys (7)
Irvinestown Primary School, Irvinestown

Shoes

Trainers, sandals, gym shoes, boots
Leather and strong
Crunching through autumn leaves
Walking, hiking, skipping along
Large and pointed, small and round
Shoes are for everyone!

Emma Glover (8)
Irvinestown Primary School, Irvinestown

Dogs

Dogs, dogs, dogs
Ginger, white and black dogs
Big, small and medium dogs
Running dogs, jumping dogs and slow dogs
Sleepy dogs, barking dogs, rolling dogs
Dogs, dogs, dogs.

Alexander Dean (8)
Irvinestown Primary School, Irvinestown

Flowers - Haiku

In the garden bed
All kinds of lovely flowers
Blooming for us all.

Matthew Thompson (7)
Irvinestown Primary School, Irvinestown

Opposite Poem

I am happy when I get sweets
I am sad when I get none
I am happy when I get a toy
I am sad when Mum says no
I am happy when I lie in
But I am sad when I have to get up.

Steven Johnston (9)
Irvinestown Primary School, Irvinestown

Butterflies

Beautiful, radiant colours
Silently flapping their wings
Fluttering on to flower heads
Tiny little insects
Nature's peaceful gift.

Rachel Law (7)
Irvinestown Primary School, Irvinestown

Diggers

Diggers, diggers, diggers
Orange, yellow, blue diggers,
Big, small, medium diggers
Shovelling, hammering, digging diggers
Levelling, spreading, scooping diggers
Diggers, diggers, diggers.

Peter Elliott (8)
Irvinestown Primary School, Irvinestown

Scramblers

Scramblers, scramblers, scramblers
Red, blue, green scramblers
Mud-climbing, rambling, stunting scramblers
Roaring, skidding, tumbling scramblers
Scramblers, scramblers, scramblers.

Joshua Crozier (7)
Irvinestown Primary School, Irvinestown

Fire

I am the master, the great
I am delighted with this scorching room
In my absence, this room is dull.

That fire extinguisher makes me shiver
In my goodness I keep you warm
You embrace in front of me
Dogs snuggle in front of me

I keep the room enlightened,
You nourish me with bundles of wood
My mouth is like an enormous cave.

Holly Johnston (10)
Irvinestown Primary School, Irvinestown

The Wind

I run swiftly round and round,
As my feet jump up and down,
With my singing, roars and whistles,
I am as fit as a fiddle,
With my roars as bold as brass,
Blowing, dancing in the grass.
As I start to fade away,
Slowly everyone comes out to play,
But tonight I will return,
Blowing round and round the park.

Amy Richmond (10)
Irvinestown Primary School, Irvinestown

Fire

I'm a beautiful flare of red, orange and gold
I spread effortlessly and rapidly
My golden glow lights up campers
Leaping from place to place
Causing mischief all around
Lit in winter homes and summer woods
Nature's flame, as bright as a ruby's glow
I roar like a giant, stomping his feet
Nothing can stop me once I start my journey
I glance at my victims in despair . . .
Victory is mine!

Jonathan Boomer (10)
Irvinestown Primary School, Irvinestown

House

I am tall and wide
Loving families inside, make me happy
They come and go
Through my gaping mouth
Spiders' webs tease as they fall
The crackling fire tickles my nose
Atishoo! Atishoo!
I protect you as you sleep
Guarding you until morning.

Edel Gallagher (10)
Irvinestown Primary School, Irvinestown

Fire

I am a roaring fire
Natural disaster
A total scare
Farmers' cows and sheep, run from me
I give light to campers.

If you annoy me, I grow big
I'll burn your house
I'll roast the trees
Don't annoy me
Always beware.

Mark Wilson (11)
Irvinestown Primary School, Irvinestown

Fire

I am very peaceful
But when I get built up with rage
I might jump at you.

Water is my foe
Oil is my friend
When I meet gas, I will explode.

I am sometimes in a cage
When I get out, I will burn the fortress down
I feed on wood.

Henry McCarthy (10)
Irvinestown Primary School, Irvinestown

Snail

A snail was on my garden path
Everywhere, even in my bath!
It leaves a trail of its own
It also has no backbone.

I call it Limey because
It's green and slimy.
It's very slow
As I'm sure you already know.

Let's have a snail race
With another snail.
We'll have fun
On that grassy place.

Now it's time to go to sleep
Say goodnight, it's time to go!
And away to sleep
He will go.

Debbie Keys (9)
Irvinestown Primary School, Irvinestown

My Friend, The Dragonfly

D own at the swamp or up in the trees,
R ound and round, whizzing through the air.
A ir is smooth, for up and down.
G oing underwater sometimes.
O pen window, coming in.
N obody disturbing me.
F lying and crawling to the habitat.
L ove the pond where I was born.
Y elling, *'Argh, a dragonfly!'*

Emma Boomer (9)
Irvinestown Primary School, Irvinestown

Minibeasts

Creepy-crawly minibeasts,
Climbing up the wall.
Small, scary minibeasts
Crawling around the hall.
Long, slimy minibeasts
Sliding under stones.
Big, biting minibeasts
Chomping through bones.
There're lots of kinds of minibeasts
Some fat and some thin.
There's even one little minibeast
In my wheelie bin!

Stewart Quinn (10)
Irvinestown Primary School, Irvinestown

Hallowe'en

H aving fun trick or treating
A pples covered in sticky toffee
L eaves are falling from the trees
L anterns and pumpkin lights shining bright
O n a dark and windy autumn night
W inter will soon be coming
E venings are drawing in
E veryone is making such a noise
N ice costumes, masks and make-up, scary faces in the dark

T rees are losing all their leaves
I n time the branches will be bare
M y mum bakes yummy apple pies
E mpty plates. 'None left!' she sighs.

Lana Knox (9)
Irvinestown Primary School, Irvinestown

Witches

Witches, witches, witches,
Ugly, warty, green witches,
Scrawny, skinny, spiny witches,
Flying, whizzing, darting witches,
Stirring, mixing, casting witches,
Witches, witches, witches.

Graeme Read (9)
Irvinestown Primary School, Irvinestown

Fudge

My dog Fudge is a star,
He is the best by far,
He's my number one
And he's lots of fun,
He never stops barking,
And never stops growling,
He likes to chew toys
And makes lots of noise,
He is white and very bright,
He's the best dog in my sight.

Jane Funston (9)
Irvinestown Primary School, Irvinestown

Hallowe'en Night!

Witches come out in the night,
The ghosts give me a fright.
Vampires coming from their graves,
Bats coming from their caves.
Spiders on their webs,
Other kids in their beds.
The moon is shining bright,
Mum said it's alright.
All it is, is Hallowe'en night!

Danielle Walker (10)
Irvinestown Primary School, Irvinestown

Autumn

Autumn is trees changing colour,
Autumn is birds migrating,
Autumn is nuts on the trees,
Autumn is berries in the bushes,
Autumn is big piles of falling leaves,
Autumn is Hallowe'en, with witches,
Autumn is fireworks going off,
Autumn is ghostly fun!

Maeve McCann (8)
Irvinestown Primary School, Irvinestown

Spider

Fat little body,
Round little head,
Eight legs long,
Was under my bed!

Into the window,
Across the sill,
Into the corner,
Ready to kill!

A silvery web,
It's spun so fast,
A deadly trap,
No fly got past!

David Knox (9)
Irvinestown Primary School, Irvinestown

My Little Brother

My little brother is
huggable and tuggable
he likes to be fed
but only in bed.

My little brother
doesn't want to play
he doesn't want to do
anything all day.

My little brother
has a chair
but if you go over
he will stare.

My little brother
likes to stare
stare at me eating
my pear.

Mark Miller (9)
Irvinestown Primary School, Irvinestown

Little Beasts And Bugs

It's funny how beetles
And creatures like that,
Can walk upside down,
As well as walk flat.

Spiders can scuttle,
Snails slide and glide,
Butterflies flutter
And caterpillars crawl.

Some people don't like them,
But I have to say,
Minibeasts and bugs,
I like them all.

Daryl Holden (8)
Irvinestown Primary School, Irvinestown

Hallowe'en

Hallowe'en comes late in the year,
When it's dark early
And witches appear,
People dressed up
And having fun,
Eating lots of food,
Watch out,
You'd better run!

All the sweets,
You will eat,
Eat, eat, eat
And trick or treat!

Rebecca Gray (9)
Irvinestown Primary School, Irvinestown

Spider!

Climbing down my bath,
Going down the plughole,
Spinning around my bed,
Round and round,
Up and down,
Just never stops.

Some spiders get stuck and never come up,
Pouncing on my head,
Inside and outside all day,
Rolling on her web, twisting and turning,
Ever seen a spider? Then you know what I mean,
Racing up and down!

Holly Walker (9)
Irvinestown Primary School, Irvinestown

Roaring Fire

I am blazing in the dark woodland,
Leaping from one place to another,
Glancing over mountainsides,
Faster than a hare.

I hear the echoing sirens,
Coming along, now the busiest lanes,
The lights first, as red as blood,
Then as blue as sapphire,
All closing in.

Water, coming faster than bullets,
I twist and turn,
Jump and dive,
He tries to follow,
But I thrive.

My foe bounces off trees,
Stumbles over branches,
As I dodge and jump,
I finally give up,
But I'll be back!

Nathan Richmond (10)
Irvinestown Primary School, Irvinestown

Fire

I am roaring hot.
With arms and legs frantically climbing,
A face like the Devil,
Eyes as red as blood,
I have teeth as sharp as knives,
I am as strong as a diamond.

I sound like thunder.
Like someone drumming loudly,
Talking very dull,
Crackling everywhere I go.

I beam out lots of light,
For people in their houses.
Dogs doze in my warm glow,
Faithful friends forever.

Nothing at all can stop me drumming.
Nothing at all can stop me burning.
Nothing can stop me. Nothing
                    Nothing
                         Nothing!

Scotty Thompson (11)
Irvinestown Primary School, Irvinestown

Snow

Snow is falling all around us
Children playing, having fun
Making snow angels and
Throwing snowballs in the air.

The neighbourhood is covered
In crystal-white
My scarf is pulled over
Very tightly.

In the evening I come
Back in and Mum
Gives me soup
I take it up to my bedroom.

I watch the snowflakes
As I am tucked up in bed.

Claudia Kelly (8)
Mount St Catherine's Primary School, Armagh

My Trampoline

I have a trampoline
I bounce very high
I do handstands
I can do flip-overs too
It's really exciting to
Be on your own
When I bounce
I feel the butterflies
Inside my tummy
I bounce high, high
Very high, into
The blue sky.

Nadine Murtagh (8)
Mount St Catherine's Primary School, Armagh

My Baby Cousin

My baby cousin
Is very cute
She always smiles
And always laughs
At my funny faces.

She jumps up and down
When she see me
She likes me very much.

Emma Kelly (8)
Mount St Catherine's Primary School, Armagh

About The School

I love science
But it's hard work.
Reading
Is good
But lots of tests
I love writing
It's the best.

But lots of homework
That's no fun
But how about PE?
It's great fun!

Abigail Quigley (9)
Mount St Catherine's Primary School, Armagh

My Baby Brother

My baby brother
I love him so much.

I kiss him and hug him
To show my love.

I hear him laughing
With joy when I come
He's talking and screaming
For my mum.

I see him jumping with joy
By the way, he's a baby boy.

Eimear Grimley (9)
Mount St Catherine's Primary School, Armagh

School Time

School time's here
Children playing, laughing, shouting
Hooray, people falling, crying.

The bell has rung
Children run to get into line first
The teacher comes
Away we go, into the classroom
We start our work, until dinner time
Then we have lots of fun in PE
Now it is dinner time
Our teacher is fun.
Now it is home time
We say goodbye to all our friends and teacher.

Maureen O'Hara (9)
Mount St Catherine's Primary School, Armagh

Roses In The Garden

Roses here
Roses there
A rose's scent
In the air
I can see
All the colours
Red, white
Yellow and blue.

Red is for love
White is for happiness
Yellow is for brightness
And blue is for you.

Catherine Marley (8)
Mount St Catherine's Primary School, Armagh

Our School

I really like going to school,
I think it's really cool!
I learn to read,
I learn to write,
I practise my numbers
Both day and night.
I love to play with my friends,
And I'm always sad when
Our break time ends!
My mummy says that school
Is a happy place to be,
And with her, I really do agree!
My school is the best ever . . .
You see!

Órla Reavey (8)
St Joseph's Primary School, Crossgar

My School

My school is St Joseph's
It is so cool
My friends are so kind to me
And the teachers are too!
My class is P4
And from September to June
I just can't wait to come in
The door.

Dervla McCormick
St Joseph's Primary School, Crossgar

Our School

The school bell rings at nine,
Just in time for me to get in line.
Then we march off to class,
Saying hello to everyone we pass.
At break time, we run around,
Having fun in the playground.
Then it's back to class again,
To learn some more, what a pain.
I really do love my school,
My classmates are so cool.
My teachers are really great,
Even when I come in late.

Donal O'Toole (7)
St Joseph's Primary School, Crossgar

My School

My school is wonderful,
I have some lovely friends.
I will be here until it suddenly begins to end.
Our school is painted blue,
It looks very nice.
Someone else will come inside,
Don't worry, there are no mice.
Our teacher is Mrs McGrath,
She is very kind,
I work very hard in class
And read my mind.

Niamh McErlane (8)
St Joseph's Primary School, Crossgar

Our School

There is a place in Crossgar
Where lots of boys and girls go
The name of this special place is
St Joseph's Primary School.
This is the place where I go to learn
My name is Christopher Martin
And this is my school
My teacher's name is Mrs McGrath.
She teaches me how to read and write
And everything to do with maths
At break time I like to run and play
Just my friends and me.
I am very happy at St Joseph's
Because it's such a fun place to be!

Christopher Martin (7)
St Joseph's Primary School, Crossgar

Our School

My school is big,
We have lots of fun.
My teacher is nice,
She helps me with my work.
We learn from our books,
How to do our work every day.
At lunchtime we have fun,
In the playground.
I have friends,
We all play together.

Daniel Martin
St Joseph's Primary School, Crossgar

Our School

My school is the best,
Because I love my spelling test.
We work so hard,
All day long.
Before we know it,
We're all singing a song!

Aileen Mahon (7)
St Joseph's Primary School, Crossgar

Autumn

Autumn is a lovely time of year.
The leaves fall to the ground.
A path of colourful leaves,
All red, brown, orange, yellow and gold.
Squirrels running round for nuts,
Up and down branches all day long.
What a lovely sight,
Grass snakes slithering about.
Field mice running round the barn for corn,
Owls sleeping in the trees.

Lisa Galligan (9)
St Martin's Primary School, Garrison

Joy

Joy is blue like a shiny, glistening sea,
Joy sounds like laughter from a small baby boy,
It tastes like chocolate melting in your mouth
And feels like a bed in a hotel suite

It reminds you of home and your family there,
Joy looks like a person willing to care,
Joy is happiness and fun,
Now my poem is finally done.

Thomas McHugh (9)
St Martin's Primary School, Garrison

Autumn

Autumn time is here again,
The nights are getting long.
The leaves have changed from green to orange
And soon they will be gone.

The animals are gathering their winter supplies,
At Hallowe'en we trick or treat
And hope there'll be no ghostly surprise!

Kilian Gilroy (11)
St Martin's Primary School, Garrison

Autumn

In the autumn, the leaves fall,
Yellow, orange, brown and green,
Oh, what is autumn without trees?
Animals getting ready for winter;
Collecting nuts and leaves,
The trees are bare;
Dressing up for Hallowe'en,
Trick or treating, getting sweets or money!

Ruth Leonard (9)
St Martin's Primary School, Garrison

In Your Dreams

I don't believe in ghosts you meet
I think it is people putting holes in a sheet

Down in the basement is where I hang out
With Dracula, whose teeth are sticking out

When witches fly so high and sing, hee, hee aloud
Rain starts to bash down from a big black cloud

Children wear costumes, knock on doors and give you a fright
Oh gosh! It sounds scary on Hallowe'en night

Do you think Hallowe'en is scary, please tell me why?
Why do people let off fireworks,
Because it makes my cats cry?

I now look at my cat when she cries
And I thank the Lord it is only lies!

Clodagh Treacy (9)
St Martin's Primary School, Garrison

Autumn

Summer has gone and autumn is here
Cold and rain is oh, so near
Short, dull days and long, dark nights
Hallowe'en and all its frights
Flowers are dying all around
Brown, dead leaves all over the ground
Yes, indeed, autumn's here
But it only comes once a year!

Roisin Flanagan (9)
St Martin's Primary School, Garrison

Autumn

In autumn
The weather is a breeze
All the leaves fall off the trees
We put our clocks an hour back
So we have an extra hour in bed
Some animals hibernate
And birds, like swallows, go and migrate!

Gillian Carson (10)
St Martin's Primary School, Garrison

Autumn

So gently they fall and rustle around,
The leaves of trees are falling to the ground.
So gently they flitter and float and play,
They all fall off on a windy autumn day.
They play around all day long,
Then they stop when the wind is gone.
The days get colder, the nights get long,
Everybody listens as the wind gets strong.
Then, when all the trees are bare,
People rake leaves up everywhere.
When everyone is playing in snow,
You will know that autumn is gone.
But do not cry or shed any tears,
Because Christmas is here -
Everyone's favourite time of year!

Ruairí Maguire (10)
St Martin's Primary School, Garrison

Autumn

All the leaves are turning shades of brown.
The windy days will blow them down.
Boys gather conkers that have fallen to the ground.
Squirrels gather nuts and berries without a sound.
They're to eat when winter comes around.

Dan Keaney (10)
St Martin's Primary School, Garrison

Autumn Leaves

Twisting, twirling through the air,
Autumn leaves are everywhere.

Red, yellow, gold and green,
On the ground they can be seen.

Rustling, crunching is the sound,
As we walk along the ground.

Wet and soggy they are to touch,
We have to sweep them with the brush.

Autumn leaves are everywhere,
But the trees are very bare.

All the leaves are dead and gone,
Many lie on our lawn.

Rosemary McGowan (10)
St Martin's Primary School, Garrison

Autumn

Leaves are falling on the ground
Leaves are falling, crisp and brown
Daddy says they clog things up
So he gets a brush and sweeps them up
The wind blows all around his face
And blows the leaves all over the place!

Ciara Flanagan (9)
St Martin's Primary School, Garrison

Love

Love is purple like a forest of bluebells,
Love sounds like a robin chirping in a tree,
Love tastes like a red, juicy apple,
Love smells like the rosiest red flower,
Love looks like the red rose growing in your garden,
Love feels like a warm place,
Love reminds me of my family and my baby cousin, Callum.

Katie Clancy (9)
St Martin's Primary School, Garrison

Love

Love is red like my dad's Ferrari.
It sounds like something popping.
It tastes like chips and pizza.
It smells like a lovely, lovely red rose.
It looks like my teacher's smile.
It feels like friendship.
It reminds me of my family.

Elaine Rooney (9)
St Martin's Primary School, Garrison

Leaves Falling

Leaves falling in the autumn time
And they change colour and fall
The days become bitter cold
After that, the trees stand bare and tall

Some trees keep their leaves
So they're called evergreen
When the snow falls later on
They'll set a nice winter scene

Nuts and berries cover the branches
Sycamore keys come spiralling down
The guelder rose has fire-red berries
Hazel and chestnuts cover the ground.

Sarah Treacy (9)
St Martin's Primary School, Garrison

Autumn Poem

In the autumn, trees are tall and colourful,
Leaves begin to fall.

In the autumn, it's getting dark
And angry dogs begin to bark, when fireworks spark.

In the autumn, Hallowe'en appears,
It brings out your true fears.

Like ghosts and goblins, there's many more,
If the Grim Reaper gets you, your arm will be sore!

In the autumn, it's very cold,
So always wear warm clothes!

Keith Keegan (9)
St Martin's Primary School, Garrison

Warship

Warship
Speed propellers
Sailing around the world
Navy people with guns
Aiming rockets away
Ready . . . aim
Fire!

Matthew Manley (9)
St Patrick's Primary School, Ballynahinch

Belina

Belina
Little rascal
Big puppy eyes
Crying, yapping, growling puppy
Playing, biting, jumping
Night-night
Puppy.

Keava Blaney (8)
St Patrick's Primary School, Ballynahinch

Puppies

Puppies
Cute, adorable
Begging, rolling, playing
Yawning, growling, crying
Small, black, cuddly
Running, eating
Puppies.

Hannah Magowan (8)
St Patrick's Primary School, Ballynahinch

Dolphins

Swimming, splashing
Big, fattish, wettish
Saving people from sharks
Jumping, diving, playing
Diving underwater
Eeek!

Rachael Walsh (8)
St Patrick's Primary School, Ballynahinch

Friends

Having fun
Seven of them
Always talking together
Sharing some secrets
Sleeping over
Asleep.

Rachel Jones (8)
St Patrick's Primary School, Ballynahinch

Birds

Chirping, flapping
All day long
Colourful feathers, all kinds
Building nests with
Sticks and branches
Birds.

Cathryn Baker (8)
St Patrick's Primary School, Ballynahinch

Lambs

Cute, cuddly
Small, bright animals
Fluffy, bleating, yapping, crying
Enjoying their lives
Frolicking, playing
Snooze.

Nicole McKay (8)
St Patrick's Primary School, Ballynahinch

My Auntie's Favourite Colour Is Pink

My auntie's favourite colour is pink,
At the weekend she has a drink,
When there is nothing on TV
She watches 'The Weakest Link',
Now and then she gives me a wink,
So my auntie's favourite colour is pink.

Tara Orr (9)
St Patrick's Primary School, Ballynahinch

My Hamster Pebbles

My hamster Pebbles is a wonderful pet,
Even when he goes to the vet.
Pebbles is black and he has a white nose,
He also has giant, pink toes.
Pebbles chews on everything he sees
And I always say, 'Don't do that, please.'
He even chews on his cage
And that really makes me rage.
I love my hamster Pebbles so very much,
He really does have a hamster's touch.

Conor Smyth-Small (10)
St Patrick's Primary School, Ballynahinch

County Down

There is a place called Down
It's all covered in trees
Everyone drinks
Everyone laughs
Everyone is happy
It is a magnificent place!

Liam Doherty (10)
St Patrick's Primary School, Ballynahinch

School

School can be good, school can be bad
I can come and go happy, or I can come and go sad
My friends like school because they see me
And if I were them, I'd most definitely agree
We all like our teachers, when they're very nice
But if we see them lose it, we should really think twice
I think English is great, I'd say the same for maths
But if I had to pick my favourite, I'd choose arts and crafts
Sometimes, in school I really want to stay
Most of the time, it's a relief to get away
Kids in school are always quite cool,
I'm glad to be in school *(sometimes)!*

Katy Flanagan (9)
St Patrick's Primary School, Ballynahinch

The Annoying Family

My brothers are the worst!
Christopher likes to dig,
He also eats like a pig.
Stephen's just a know-it-all,
He never hoovers in the hall.
Then, Mum just hates flies,
Her room is like a pigsty.
Then Dad can really shout,
You disagree, he'll throw you out.
Some people think Ryan's the best,
When he's really just an annoying pest.
It's the wee boy, Ryan's, time to shine,
The best thing about this family, well it's mine!

Ryan Molloy (9)
St Patrick's Primary School, Ballynahinch

My Best Friends

Friends, friends, wonderful friends,
Happy, sad friends,
They run and play every day.
Happy, happy, happy friends,
Best friends are always there
Happy, sad, anytime
My best friends are Lauren and you
And that's the end of my best friends!

Natasha McMillan (10)
St Patrick's Primary School, Ballynahinch

Amazing Autumn

In autumn I watch leaves turn red, orange and gold
In the wind they twist, turn and fold
I hear leaves under my wellies, crunching
What a huge pie I could be munching

I smell the warm, crisp air
Look at the foxes snuggle down in their lair
Feel the soft touch of the squirrel
Through the trees, he twists and twirls

Think of autumn, think in your mind
My tongue feels like it will wind
How many other autumn fruits I may find
I taste the berries, my mouth waters

Look at the fruits, leaves and colours you can find
Autumn fruits, taste the blackberries
Their flavour nice? Yes, very, very
Every leaf we find each day
Shows that autumn's on its way!

Katie Hughes (7)
St Patrick's Primary School, Dungannon

Winter

W inter is so cold and white
 I nside a deep dark hole are little dormice sleeping
 N ow the day has passed, don't light the fire, Santa Claus will be set on fire!
 T oday it is cold, icy and windy, don't go outside
 E normous snowman in everybody's gardens
 R ent a DVD and watch it with me.

Carrie Coary (8)
St Patrick's Primary School, Dungannon

Spring Days

Spring days are very nice
Lambs are being born
The days are getting longer, the nights are getting shorter

It doesn't rain as it used to
Smell the fresh sky
My cold lollies are in the fridge
Waiting for me to lick them!

Anna Maguire (7)
St Patrick's Primary School, Dungannon

Change

I can hear the rustling leaves in the autumn wind.
I can taste the juicy fruits of autumn watering in my mouth.
I can touch the gold and red leaves as they softly fall on the ground.
I can smell the burning bonfire on Hallowe'en night.
I can see that it is autumn as I see change all around.

Peter Kelly (7)
St Patrick's Primary School, Dungannon

Autumn

In autumn I watch leaves fall off the trees.
The colours are red, orange, gold and yellow.
In the wind they twist and twirl everywhere.
I hear leaves under my wellies, crunching.
There are lots of leaves in autumn.

Ciaran McAllister (7)
St Patrick's Primary School, Dungannon

Spring

I can see the beautiful birds in the sky.
I can hear the beautiful wind blow.
I can smell the beautiful flowers.
I can touch the beautiful green leaves.
I can taste beautiful spring.

Chloe Fitzpatrick (7)
St Patrick's Primary School, Dungannon

Autumn Time

I can feel the crunch of the leaves under my feet.
Sometimes when I am cold, I sit in my seat.

I can see the leaves fall off the tree onto the ground.
When you are looking for them, they can be found.

I can smell the berries on the bushes.
Sometimes my brother pushes.

I can taste the pie that my mum makes.
Sometimes my brother's sick but sometimes he fakes.

I can touch the leaves on the ground.
When you try to catch them, they blow around.

Dearbhla Rafferty (7)
St Patrick's Primary School, Dungannon

Autumn

When I go outside, I see the leaves falling from the sky
I try and catch them but they blow in the wind
And they land on the ground.
When I go inside, the trees blow in the wind.
It sounds like water falling from the sky
And the leaves that are gold look like money.

Eoin O'Hagan (7)
St Patrick's Primary School, Dungannon

Summer

In summer the trees have green leaves
The children go back to school
The days are hotter
People wear sunglasses
We eat ice cream
Farmers shear their sheep
People go on holidays
The farmers let the cows out into the fields
The farmers also harvest their crops.

Darryl Mullan (8)
St Patrick's Primary School, Dungannon

In Autumn

Leaves change colour and drop onto the cold ground.
Cold, windy and wet weather when winter is near.
Animals get ready to hibernate by collecting nuts and berries.
Children jump in the leaves.
We wear warmer clothes.
Waiting for the snow to drop!

Caoimhe Shields (8)
St Patrick's Primary School, Dungannon

Sunny Days

S unny days, playing about, having a shout
U nder the trees, in the shade
M ost children off school
M y friends have holidays
E ating ice cream from the cone, it's very nice
R unning around, hearing children play.

Cormac McGhee (7)
St Patrick's Primary School, Dungannon

Winter

W hen it was winter it snowed, it snowed
 I t snowed like hell and I shouted, *'Hooray!'*
N ow, when it's Christmas, Santa Claus comes down
T he chimney and leaves some presents for the children
E ating cookies when we get up in the morning
R ace you down the stairs!

Toni Morris (7)
St Patrick's Primary School, Dungannon

Winter

I can smell the fire burning.
I can taste the hot chocolate running down my throat.
I can see the white snowballs going past.
I can hear the silence of the winter.
I can touch the freezing cold ice.

Callum Donnelly (7)
St Patrick's Primary School, Dungannon

Summer

S ummer is a lovely season and the sun always shines
U se the cold drink in the jug if you get too warm
M y daddy hates the summer, he says he is allergic
M y mummy's favourite season is summer
E arly in the morning, I can hear the baby birds
R abbits hopping around - I wish I had one.

Donovan McNeil (8)
St Patrick's Primary School, Dungannon

Autumn Days

Autumn days are very short, but the nights are long and dark
When we go outside to play, I wrap up tight and try to keep warm.

Up into the sky the kites go, as I run along the hill,
In the park with my warmest hat on.

Times goes by and I get tired and thirsty
I go home to have a cup of tea.

Upon the ground the leaves lie
With dirty, beautiful colours.

My mummy's apple pie burns in my mouth.
Nine winter roses in my mummy's best vase.

Aideen Duffy (7)
St Patrick's Primary School, Dungannon

Spring

S pring is a really nice and colourful season
P eople like to play outside when it is not raining
R ain makes the flowers colourful and it also makes them grow
I love spring
N ow, baby lambs are born
G et a big spring-clean!

Philip Barrett (7)
St Patrick's Primary School, Dungannon

On A Sunny Day
(Inspired by 'On a Breezy Day' by Iain Crichton-Smith)

On a sunny day
The sun looks like a ball of fire
It feels cosy on my skin
The sea soaks up its heat
Like a sponge.

Bebhinn Stuart (7)
SS Patrick & Brigid's Primary School, Ballycastle

On A Cloudy Day
(Inspired by 'On a Breezy Day' by Iain Crichton-Smith)

On a cloudy day
The clouds look like
A soft pillow
Lying on a bed of soft
White snow.

Liam Fletcher (8)
SS Patrick & Brigid's Primary School, Ballycastle

On A Windy Day
(Inspired by 'On a Breezy Day' by Iain Crichton-Smith)

On a windy day
The leaves rustle on the trees like mad
As if they were alive
And the curtains blow out the window like
Different coloured lightning flashing out of the sky
The sand on the beach blows up
Into your eyes.

Toraigh Watson (8)
SS Patrick & Brigid's Primary School, Ballycastle

On A Sunny Day
(Inspired by 'On a Breezy Day' by Iain Crichton-Smith)

On a sunny day
The sun can seem different colours
Like orange and yellow.
The sun sets at night-time
And the stars come out to shine.

Laura Duigan (8)
SS Patrick & Brigid's Primary School, Ballycastle

On A Windy Day
(Inspired by 'On a Breezy Day' by Iain Crichton-Smith)

On a windy day
The trees blow like a bendy rubber
And the wind blows the leaves about
And it is really cold.

Émer McBride (7)
SS Patrick & Brigid's Primary School, Ballycastle

On A Sunny Day
(Inspired by 'On a Breezy Day' by Iain Crichton-Smith)

On a sunny day
The ice cream melts
Dripping down the cone
Like snow falling to the ground.

Eoin McCaughan (7)
SS Patrick & Brigid's Primary School, Ballycastle

On A Snowy Day
(Inspired by 'On a Breezy Day' by Iain Crichton-Smith)

On a snowy day
The snow lands on the earth
Like tiny snowmen
Coming from Heaven.

Aisha McAuley (7)
SS Patrick & Brigid's Primary School, Ballycastle

On A Sunny Day
(Inspired by 'On a Breezy Day' by Iain Crichton-Smith)

On a sunny day
The dust flies through the air
Like tiny stars
Falling from the sky.

Pearse Molloy (7)
SS Patrick & Brigid's Primary School, Ballycastle

On A Foggy Day
(Inspired by 'On a Breezy Day' by Iain Crichton-Smith)

On a foggy day
Things disappear
As if a magician
Has cast a spell on them.

Georgie Killough (7)
SS Patrick & Brigid's Primary School, Ballycastle

On A Windy Day
(Inspired by 'On a Breezy Day' by Iain Crichton-Smith)

On a windy day
a tree falls down
and curves like a bridge
over a river.

Bronagh Scullion (7)
SS Patrick & Brigid's Primary School, Ballycastle

On A Windy Day
(Inspired by 'On a Breezy Day' by Iain Crichton-Smith)

On a windy day
The wind blows like a burst balloon.
It can turn over a car
Or turn off the power.

Tiarnan Jennings (8)
SS Patrick & Brigid's Primary School, Ballycastle

On A Stormy Day
(Inspired by 'On a Breezy Day' by Iain Crichton-Smith)

On a stormy day
the storm smashes and crashes
like an angry master.
It can be scary
until it calms down
leaving behind a big
wrecked city.

Conor Mullan (7)
SS Patrick & Brigid's Primary School, Ballycastle

The Snowflakes Falling From The Moon's Pocket
(Inspired by 'On a Breezy Day' by Iain Crichton-Smith)

On a snowy day
The snowflakes fall from the sky
Like white glitter
From the moon's pockets.

Caolan Hill (7)
SS Patrick & Brigid's Primary School, Ballycastle

On A Snowy Day
(Inspired by 'On a Breezy Day' by Iain Crichton-Smith)

On a snowy day
the snowflakes
drift down from the sky
like shining stars
falling onto the Earth.

Alex McMullan (7)
SS Patrick & Brigid's Primary School, Ballycastle

Bright Trees
(Inspired by 'On a Breezy Day' by Iain Crichton-Smith)

On a sunny day
the trees shine brightly
but sometimes dark
like a picture
drawn by an artist.

Chloe Woods (7)
SS Patrick & Brigid's Primary School, Ballycastle

The Man In The Garden
(Inspired by 'On a Breezy Day' by Iain Crichton-Smith)

On a snowy day
The snowman
Sits in the garden
Like a white man
With snowflakes falling all around.

Caitlin Winchborne (7)
SS Patrick & Brigid's Primary School, Ballycastle

On A Snowy Day
(Inspired by 'On a Breezy Day' by Iain Crichton-Smith)

On a snowy day
Snow drops, drifts down
It looks like glitter in the sky.

Caoimhe Marie Donnelly (7)
SS Patrick & Brigid's Primary School, Ballycastle#

On A Snowy Day
(Inspired by 'On a Breezy Day' by Iain Crichton-Smith)

On a snowy day
The snowflakes drifted down from the glittery sky
Like golden stars from the sky onto the ground
And when the last snowflake fell from the sky
All the snowflakes turned into
A warm blanket over the Earth.

Clodagh McFaul (7)
SS Patrick & Brigid's Primary School, Ballycastle

On A Snowy Day
(Inspired by 'On a Breezy Day' by Iain Crichton-Smith)

On a snowy day
Children play and throw snowballs
Like cannonballs shooting
Through the air.

Ryan Davidson (8)
SS Patrick & Brigid's Primary School, Ballycastle

On A Stormy Day
(Inspired by 'On a Breezy Day' by Iain Crichton-Smith)

On a stormy day
The waves banged against the lighthouse
Like an angry monster
It was bright outside
I had to play on that day
It wasn't nice.

Cara Kinney (7)
SS Patrick & Brigid's Primary School, Ballycastle

A Snowy Day
(Inspired by 'On a Breezy Day' by Iain Crichton-Smith)

On a snowy day
The snowdrops
Flutter down to the ground
And cover the world
With a snowy blanket.

Ben Large (8)
SS Patrick & Brigid's Primary School, Ballycastle

A Snowy Day
(Inspired by 'On a Breezy Day' by Iain Crichton-Smith)

On a snowy day the snowflakes
Danced to the ground.
The snow settled on the earth
Like a white blanket.
It's like falling stars from the sky
And you can play in the snow!

Caoimhe Norwood (7)
SS Patrick & Brigid's Primary School, Ballycastle

On A Snowy Day
(Inspired by 'On a Breezy Day' by Iain Crichton-Smith)

On a snowy day
Snowflakes drifted
Down from the sky.
It was like raindrops coming down
From the bright sky.
It came down to the ground like
Shooting stars coming down from the white sky.
It looked like glitter coming down
From the sky's pocket.

Cailín Haughey (7)
SS Patrick & Brigid's Primary School, Ballycastle

A Snowy Day
(Inspired by 'On a Breezy Day' by Iain Crichton-Smith)

On a snowy day
Snow falls on the green
And it covers the world in a cold blanket
Like a big avalanche coming down.

Patrick Bonnar (7)
SS Patrick & Brigid's Primary School, Ballycastle

The Leaves Fall From The Trees
(Inspired by 'On a Breezy Day' by Iain Crichton-Smith)

On a windy day
The leaves sway on the trees.
They fall from the heavens to the ground
Like little helicopters falling from the sky.

Logan McLean (8)
SS Patrick & Brigid's Primary School, Ballycastle

Sunny
(Inspired by 'On a Breezy Day' by Iain Crichton-Smith)

The sun is like a diamond in the sky
It sparkles its light down on the town
When it feels tired it goes to bed
And wakes up the moon.

Shannon McDermott (7)
SS Patrick & Brigid's Primary School, Ballycastle

On A Sunny Day
(Inspired by 'On a Breezy Day' by Iain Crichton-Smith)

The sun is shaped
like a disco ball.
It sprinkles and glitters
in the sky.

Shannon McGrogan (7)
SS Patrick & Brigid's Primary School, Ballycastle

On A Windy Day
(Inspired by 'On a Breezy Day' by Iain Crichton-Smith)

On a windy day
The leaves fly over your head
Fall gently on the ground
And they make a quilt.

Ruthie Burns (7)
SS Patrick & Brigid's Primary School, Ballycastle

Autumn Fun

I see leaves on the enormous trees,
I feel very wet grass,
I smell lovely apple pie,
I hear birds singing away
While flying to a different land,
I taste the lovely black and blue berries.

Mark Conroy (8)
Towerview Primary School, Bangor

Hallowe'en Night

I can see ghosts and leaves going past my bedroom window.
I can hear the birds flying away somewhere else.
I can smell my cookies for supper cooking in the oven.
I can feel the cookies before I eat them.
I can taste the yummy cookies in my mouth!

Shannon Palnoch (7)
Towerview Primary School, Bangor

Autumn

I see flowers in autumn
I hear the birds chirping
I touch a delicious blueberry
I taste a juicy blackberry
I smell a beautiful red flower.

Hannah Tuson (8)
Towerview Primary School, Bangor

Hallowe'en Fun

I can see all the people go by in their scary costumes,
I can hear the toffee apple crunching in my mouth,
I can smell the leather costume I'm going to wear,
I can taste the lovely chocolate melting in my mouth,
I can touch a smooth pumpkin.

Phoebe Preston (7)
Towerview Primary School, Bangor

Autumn Fun

In autumn leaves fall off the trees
At Hallowe'en we go to any door we see,
I hear birds singing in the trees,
I can touch blackberries in autumn,
I can smell apple pie in autumn,
I can taste blueberry pie.

Nicholas Price (7)
Towerview Primary School, Bangor

Autumn Fun

I can see the leaves falling from the trees,
I can taste the blackberry, very sweet,
I can touch the autumn beat,
I can smell the wind as well,
I can hear the little bird singing on the pier.

Tamsyn Cummins (7)
Towerview Primary School, Bangor

Autumn Fun

I can see leaves, all sorts of colours, red, green, yellow
I can hear the dead leaves when I stand on them
I can touch cotton wool all soft and cuddly
I can touch leaves that are sometimes rough.
I can taste sweets and berries, they are nice.
I can smell the strawberries.

Lucy Blaney (7)
Towerview Primary School, Bangor

Hallowe'en

I see the pumpkins all about.
Some kids I hear down the street
Saying, 'Trick or treat?'
I can touch the plastic of a costume.
I can taste pumpkin pie, yummy.
I can smell fireworks.
They remind me of flames.

Melanie Sloan (7)
Towerview Primary School, Bangor

Autumn Senses

I see birds flying to hotter countries in autumn,
I see the wind carrying the brown and green leaves,
I hear leaves crunch when I walk on them,
I hear the wind banging on my postbox,
I like to touch all the slimy and crunchy bugs,
I like to touch the cold and icy water,
I like to taste the yummy blueberries,
I like to taste the yummy jam,
I like to smell the nice smell of the flowers,
I like to smell the delicious smell of blueberries.

Connor Firth (7)
Towerview Primary School, Bangor

In The Autumn Time

I see the fireworks up so high,
The colours fill up the sky,
I see the leaves fall to the ground,
Ruby-red, amber and brown,
I watch the birds singing in the trees,
I smell the gentle autumn breeze,
The blackberries taste sweet,
The apples are fresh,
I hear my friends playing in the leaves,
I touch the damp grass.

Rhiannon Wells (8)
Towerview Primary School, Bangor

I Like

I like to see fireworks lighting up the sky
They are bright colours
Red, blue, indigo, gold, silver
They are brilliant.
I can hear *crackle, bang, twitch*
Exploding fireworks going off in circles
Loops and twirls.

Then at midnight when I hear a wicked witch
Touch the window with her long bony fingers,
It frightens me.

At Hallowe'en, I like to taste pumpkin pie.
It is sweet.
I like the smell of fireworks going off.
It smells of fire.

Nathan James Connor Ritchie (8)
Towerview Primary School, Bangor

Autumn Sense Poem

I touch the smooth brown conkers,
Hear the lovely fireworks go boom,
Shining colours like red and orange,
Watch smoke cover the sky grey,
Smell the lovely sweet toffee apples,
See the lovely, sparkling, tweeting birds,
Taste the lovely sweet apples.

Jordan Thompson (7)
Towerview Primary School, Bangor

Autumn Sense Poem

Hear the kids
Laughing and shouting
'Trick or treat?' and
Running round the street
Taste the candy all different sorts,
Caramel and toffee apples.
See the smiling faces of children
Looking up at the stars.
Smell the bonfire's smoke
As it covers the sky.
Touch the rough skin of a pumpkin.

Joshua Doherty (7)
Towerview Primary School, Bangor

The Wind

W histling wind in the trees
I n the night when all sleeps the wind is awake and watching you
N ever-ending gusts of wind that take you by surprise
D umbfounded as this may seem the wind is your friend.

Rebecca McCormick (10)
Towerview Primary School, Bangor

Autumn

A utumn is a colourful season
U nderneath trees, the leaves float down
T he leaves turn into warm colours
U p into the breezy sky, clouds will pass by
M any animals hibernate and birds migrate
N ow get up off your chair, go outside and explore
                                     the sparkly fireworks!

Erin Rachel Moore (10)
Towerview Primary School, Bangor

The Wind

The strong, blustery gale is blowing,
All trees are shivering,
While they lose their warm leaf coat.

Every creature is taking shelter,
In some place warm and dry,
Knowing that the wind will die out,
And all will be safe again.

Sara McDowell (10)
Towerview Primary School, Bangor

Wind Wonders

Do you like the leaves in the wind?
I do.
Side to side blow the trees,
Oohing and wooing all night long,
Wind wonders are really strong,
Here is the good thing,
It keeps us cool,
After school,
Do you like to hear the leaves in the wind?
I do!

Portia Preston (10)
Towerview Primary School, Bangor

Autumn

Autumn leaves crunch
They are lying in a bunch
Leaves go up and down
Children don't frown
Fruit is ready to be picked off trees
Children love autumn leaves
Leaves brown, yellow and red
Children now go to bed.

Ashleigh Phillips (10)
Towerview Primary School, Bangor

Autumn

A utumn is when Hallowe'en comes, it is so exciting
U nderground animals begin to hibernate
T rick or treating is really fun getting sweets and money, it's a blast
U mbrellas go up now that summer has gone and winter is coming
M aking candy apples and cutting a face in a pumpkin it's so
                                                                                     messy to do
N ow Hallowe'en is here people are getting together and having
                                                                                    Hallowe'en parties.

Paige Morrow (10)
Towerview Primary School, Bangor

Summer Fun - Haiku

Summer's just begun,
It's time to have lots of fun,
Playing in the sun.

India McPeak (9)
Towerview Primary School, Bangor

Beach Days - Haiku

I went to the beach
I went surfing yesterday
I went to Coleraine.

Thomas Watson (8)
Towerview Primary School, Bangor

Summer Holidays - Haiku

I am at the beach
You can bodyboard all day
I just love ice cream.

Rachel Lyle (9)
Towerview Primary School, Bangor

The Block - Haiku

Summer is the best
We run around the block fast
We sing songs today.

Angus Gardiner (8)
Towerview Primary School, Bangor

Summer Fun! - Haiku

Playing on the beach,
The sun gave a big heatwave,
Summer was the best!

Chloe Budd (10)
Towerview Primary School, Bangor

Summer - Haiku

It is summertime.
It is quite hot at Benone.
I slept at Benone.

Nial Ian William Scott (8)
Towerview Primary School, Bangor

Surfing At The Beach - Haiku

Let's go to the beach
We got to the beach and surfed
We had a good time.

Israel Corry (8)
Towerview Primary School, Bangor

Travelling - Haiku

Travelling on planes
Staying in a caravan
Swimming and playing.

Jenny Huston (10)
Towerview Primary School, Bangor

Getting Wet - Haiku

Time to get wet yeah!
Skiing and jumping the wave
Going really fast.

Andrew Mellon (9)
Towerview Primary School, Bangor

Leaves

Crunchy, crunchy, sound the leaves.
See them whirl and dance.
Feel like sand in your hand.
Red, brown and gold.

Lee Puckrin (8)
Towerview Primary School, Bangor

Summertime - Haiku

It is a great day
Can we go out and play now?
I had fun playing.

Gemma McCamley (8)
Towerview Primary School, Bangor

In The Sea - Haiku

I am in the sea
Wetsuit on and bodyboard
Going really fast.

Andrew Poxon (9)
Towerview Primary School, Bangor

The Seaside Adventure - Haiku

The sun is scorching
I made a big sandcastle
I went knee boarding.

Conor Dorrian (9)
Towerview Primary School, Bangor

Fly, Fly Away - Haiku

Swimming is the best
My friend asked me to the pool
Sunbathing is cool.

Lucy McClenahan (9)
Towerview Primary School, Bangor

Hallowe'en Night

A stormy night came
Nothing was the same

'Help me, help!' I yelled
'N-o,' someone spelled.

I wonder who that was
He comes silently yes he does.

Then he said, *'Boo!'*
I remember this from Doctor Who

It was really my best friend Phil
You know, the one from the Old Windmill.

James Carson (10)
Towerview Primary School, Bangor

Autumn Sense Poem

See the spiky conkers
Look at the autumn trees
We see the leaves on the trees
The trees have red, brown and green leaves.

Alex Hannant (7)
Towerview Primary School, Bangor

Autumn

Brown and yellow and green leaves
Blowing around the ground
I love picking blackberries
On the autumn ground
I love tasting apple pie.

Natasha Mellon (7)
Towerview Primary School, Bangor

Hallowe'en

Ghosts crawling across the window
Scared me!
Help!
Help!
Mum come quickly!

Jack Maitland (7)
Towerview Primary School, Bangor

Autumn Sense Poem

Look, autumn is here!
Smell the black smoke from the bonfire.
Taste an apple from an apple tree.
See the buzzy bee fly back to its nest.
Hear the birds singing a beautiful tune
And touch the smooth berries on a bush.
Oh look, what a beautiful sight!
The fireworks with lovely colours . . .
Red, yellow, blue, purple and orange.

Zoë Elena Beckett (7)
Towerview Primary School, Bangor

Autumn Sense Poem

I can hear the fireworks explode in the air.
I can smell the burning bonfire in the field.
I can hear the birds tweeting on the trees.
I can see the conkers on the ground.

Emma Waugh (7)
Towerview Primary School, Bangor

Autumn Sense Poem

Touch a hedgehog hibernating
under a bed of leaves.
I can hear the fireworks
booming in the sky.
Taste the sweets and the candy
while you go trick or treating
with the fireworks exploding in the sky.

Matthew Adendorff (8)
Towerview Primary School, Bangor

Autumn Sense Poem

Feel the very pointy prickles of a hedgehog.
Hear all the noisy fireworks booming in the grey sky.
Taste all the different kinds of sweets.
Watch all the glowing sparklers shine about outside.
Smell all the delicious pies from other people's ovens.

James Wylie (7)
Towerview Primary School, Bangor

Autumn Sense Poem

Feel the spiky prickles
of a conker sitting on the ground.
Hear the tweeting birds
collecting food to hibernate.
See the leaves falling off the trees
and the kids kicking them in the breeze.
Smell the smoke of the shooting fireworks
sparkling all different colours in the air.
Taste the lovely toffee apples at Hallowe'en.

Dylan Robinson (7)
Towerview Primary School, Bangor

Autumn Sense Poem

Touch the smooth skin of a shiny conker.
See the wind scoop up the leaves in the shape of a tornado.
Smell the smoke from a burning bonfire.
Taste the sweets when you come home from trick or treating . . .
But! Beware of the spooky shadows.
Hear the leaves rustling as they fall from the trees.

Savannah Romein (7)
Towerview Primary School, Bangor

Autumn Sense Poem

A shining conker on the ground
Watch the flashing fireworks
Hear the yellow, brown and red leaves crunch under your feet
Taste the toffee apples on Hallowe'en night.

Chloe Neill (7)
Towerview Primary School, Bangor

Autumn Sense Poem

Touch the spiky hedgehog hibernating.
See the shining fireworks pointing into the air,
Gold, red, blue, pink and purple.
Hear the wind blowing in the sky,
Making the leaves fly away.
Taste the candy sweets and hot apple pie
From the fresh, warm oven.

Ryan Scott (7)
Towerview Primary School, Bangor

Autumn Sense Poem

Hear the leaves crack and crunch
As you stamp on the ground.
Touch your scarf for warmth in the cold air.
See the golden-brown leaves of an autumn tree.
Smell the conkers burning in the firelight.
Taste the sweets, candy and chocolate in your sack
From trick or treating.

Siân Barker (7)
Towerview Primary School, Bangor

Autumn Sense Poem

Hear fireworks screeching in the sky
While children jump in the air
Tasting candy all night long
And rustling the leaves
Touch the conkers, shiny or smooth
See the animals hibernating.

Ben McCreery (7)
Towerview Primary School, Bangor

Autumn Sense Poem

I can hear the fireworks crackle
And the Catherine wheel spinning in the air.
See the birds picking the twigs up for their nests.
Hear the baby birds cheeping on the roof.
Taste the toffee apples stuck in your teeth.

Catherine Poxon (8)
Towerview Primary School, Bangor

Autumn Sense Poem

Touch the spiky prickles of a hibernating hedgehog
Feel the smooth brown conker in its spiky case hang from a tree
Taste the sweet-smelling sweets and appley pie
Smell the smoke of fireworks booming off into the sky!

Isaac Cave (8)
Towerview Primary School, Bangor